MW01579210

Searching for the Way:
A Road Map to a Better Life

By Richard Sain

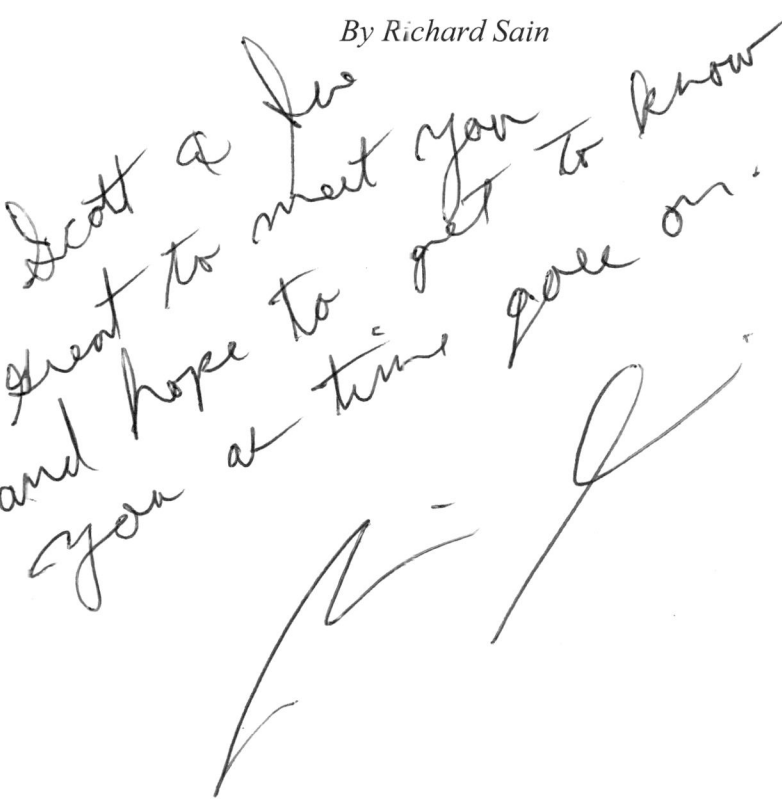

Scott a few great to meet you and hope to get to know you at time goes on.

Copyright 2012
By: Richard Sain

Christianity, if false, is of no importance, and if true, of infinite importance. The only thing it cannot be is moderately important.

- C.S. Lewis

Table of Contents

Introduction

Human beings are born to search. From early infancy we begin crawling around searching for new things. When we find them, we pick them up, examine them, analyze them, name them and experiment with them. Sometimes, these experiments can be beneficial as we make "breakthrough" discoveries. There have been a huge number of these "breakthroughs" in electronics, medical science and engineering. Now, as a result, we know more and live longer and healthier lives.

Sometimes, experiments go horribly wrong. Many people have experimented with drugs and alcohol in their lives resulting in failed marriages, physical and psychological damage and sometimes death. Yet, there is something inside each of us that is willing to take risks and experiment. The driving force is curiosity. Curiosity drives us to search. In Matthew 7:13-14 Jesus says, "Enter through the narrow gate. For wide is the gate and broad is the road that leads to destruction, and many enter through it. But small is the gate, and narrow the road that leads to life, and only a few find it."

I spent a few years walking down the broad road that leads to destruction. When I was seventeen, I began to sneak cans of beer from my mother's stash hidden under her bed. Soon afterwards, I began to smoke marijuana and then began cultivating it in our backyard. From there, I began experimenting with hashish, PCP, cocaine and LSD. From the time I turned eighteen, when I falsified my driver's license, there always a fifth of Jose Cuervo Gold sitting in my bedroom. I spent countless nights frequenting night clubs while attending college.

Ultimately, I began losing it psychologically. I became very paranoid and withdrawn and depressed. I remember walking into my room several times and literally hiding under the covers with a headset on listening to music. There was a period of time that I suffered from insomnia and ended up going on long walks at night while other people slept.

On one of those nights, an LAPD officer grabbed me from behind without identifying himself. As I was yanked around by the shoulder, I used the momentum and threw a kick into the officer's chest driving him to the ground. His partner started drawing his gun as the officer I kicked pulled me down to the ground and into a choke hold. That earned me two years probation. Another night, I heard a dachshund telling me that it wasn't her fault that she looked so ridiculously funny.

One evening, I became particularly paranoid. I was certain that FBI officers were ready to break into my home and shoot me. I tossed and turned trying to fall asleep for hours. I was totally freaking out. It suddenly dawned on me. I couldn't continue on like this. I was physically, mentally and psychologically exhausted. I needed help badly. I finally asked Jesus to help me. I told him that I had really messed up my life and needed Him to help me. I asked him into my life and begged for his mercy and forgiveness.

Finally, I had found the small gate and voluntarily walked through it and onto the narrow path. My life has never been the same. I have lived an abundant life now for 40 years. My wife and I have been married for over 30 years and we have raised four wonderful children.

The purpose of this book is to help you in your search for a better life. Hopefully, you are curious enough to take the risk and spend some time experimenting with the concepts in this book. My ultimate goal is to help you find your way onto the narrow path. So, keep on reading and follow me to the gate that leads to the narrow way!

Love Your Enemies

When I first read the following words that Jesus Christ spoke some 2,000 years ago, I could not understand the thinking behind them: "Love your enemies..." from Luke 6:32. How could I love my enemies? I had a hard enough time loving my family and friends. I hated my enemies as much as the next guy. It was the early 1970's and I had just finished my junior year at California State University at Northridge. A classmate of mine had invited me to something he called a fellowship dinner – whatever that was.

There was something different about this guy. He seemed to grasp something that had been eluding me. He was more alive than anyone else I had ever known before. I was intrigued by him, so I accepted his offer. His name was Richard and he made no excuses about being a Christian. The other participants at the dinner were equally alive and friendly. Richard and a couple of his friends were deeply concerned about the state of my being. How did they know I was so messed up?

After spending an evening with these folks, I would have trusted them with my life. So, when Richard asked me if I had ever read the Bible, I was all ears. I told him that I never read it and that I didn't even have a copy of it in my home. Richard gave me his own Bible and encouraged me to start reading the New Testament. I clutched it and immediately was determined to read it.

I had just turned 21 and somewhere deep inside of me, I knew that there was more to life than what I had been experiencing. I was on a quest to find it. I certainly hadn't found it in drugs or alcohol. I read Siddhartha, Autobiography of a Yogi, Bhagavad-Gita, and The Tibetan Book of the

Dead. These were interesting works, but they didn't do much for me.

I began reading the New Testament as Richard had suggested. His Bible was the King James Version. It was beautifully written. Having been written about 2,000 years ago, I had assumed that it was more of a historical document and couldn't really speak to me today. As I read it, I was amazed at how relevant it was. I had no idea that the Bible was written about human nature. It quickly became evident to me that human nature today, is exactly what human nature was 2,000 years ago.

People's pride and arrogance and greed and jealousy were all there and are all still with us today. In John 14:6 Jesus says: "I am the way and the truth and the life." In one sentence Jesus just summed up what I was looking for. I was lost and needed to find my way. I was searching for the truth. And I was looking for life. In John 10:10 Jesus also said: "…I have come that they may have life, and have it to the full." Again, this is what I wanted. And if Jesus was all three things wrapped up together, then I found what I had been looking for – Jesus.

As I worked my way through the New Testament, I began growing angry. After twelve years of compulsory education and three years of college, why hadn't this book been on a reading list in any of my classes? I was furious! Someone should have directed me to this treasure years ago! There was so much to be learned about life in this book! It was filled with so much wisdom and guidance on how to live. There were so many lessons about people and God.

In 1 John 4:16 I read: "God is love." After looking for love in all the wrong places, I finally found it in the Bible! Not only that, Paul, a Disciple of Jesus, defined love for us in Corinthians 13: 4-7: "Love is patient, love is kind. It does not envy, it does not boast, it is not proud. It is not rude, it is not self seeking, it is not easily angered, it keeps no records of wrongs. Love does not delight in evil, but rejoices with the truth. It always protects, always trusts, always hopes, always perseveres." Since God is love then it is also true that love is God. So, all of the above attributes of love can also be ascribed to God.

You might be wondering how I knew that there was more to life. I guess I had a piece of that love in my very being. And as Paul said above, love always hopes and always perseveres. And even if I had spent 21 years of my life living as

God's enemy, God still loved me, and had hope for me and was perseverant. In other words, God let me know that he was around.

The first time that God revealed himself to me, I was 20 years old. A friend of mine and I were about ready to return home from visiting a mutual friend of ours. It was late at night. Before leaving, God had spoken to me. It wasn't in an audible voice; it was more like instant messaging. And this was the message: "Don't sit in the front seat. Lie down on the back seat with your feet against one side of the car and place your head on your sleeping bag against the other side of the car. The car is going to roll over."

I didn't tell anyone about this message, I just obeyed it. Sure enough, the car started skidding about five minutes after we left and then violently rolled over landing on the corner of the car's roof just above the passenger seat. When I got out of the car, and saw how severely the roof had caved in over the passenger seat, I realized that my neck and back would have been crushed! Instead of dying that night, I walked away without a scratch. All I did was obey God, and he saved my life!

This was all rather bizarre. I was definitely freaked out. I started having anxiety attacks and wondered why and how this could happen. There was no logical explanation to what happened. Not having read the Bible, I was lacking the knowledge that God is love and that love always protects. Now, the words that Jesus spoke: "Love your enemies…" began to make sense. God loved me even though I was his enemy. And Jesus was telling us to do the same. He was telling us to make love our default setting. It should be our number one priority and be placed in front of and above hatred. He was telling us this for our own benefit. Hatred is an ugly and destructive emotion. It is better to love rather than to hate. There is peace in love. Hatred fills us with turmoil, negativity and disturbing thoughts.

It's easy to find people to hate. Some people hate their teachers, others hate their ex-husbands or ex-wives, and plenty of people hate their bosses. But you know what? It's not worth it! Hatred is like a festering sore that never goes away. It eats at you day and night making you miserable. It is much better to forgive those your hate and concentrate on those you love. The first step to loving your enemies is forgiving them. So, the next time you start thinking about someone you hate, tell yourself to forgive that person for what they had done and then start thinking about someone you love. Think about what positive thing you can do for that person to make their life better.

God is Love

A while back, I listened to an atheist being interviewed on National Public Radio. The man went on and on about how being an atheist was the right thing to be and how he knew it was the right thing to be and how he whole heartedly did not believe in God. He said all this in a rather emotionless manner. When he was all done spewing his opinions, the interviewer asked him a simple question: "Do you believe in Love?" The man suddenly became more animated and replied enthusiastically that indeed he believed in love and spoke of the many attributes of love. In a few sentences he completely contradicted himself in the most fervent manner!

Apparently, he never read the Bible. If he had, he would know that God is love. In 1 John 4:8 it says: "Whoever does not love, does not know

God, because God is love." So, if you believe in love, you believe in God. That interviewer, whether she knew it or not, just blew that guy's whole belief system and argument to smithereens! It brought a deep sense of joy to me. Here was a self-proclaimed atheist who acknowledged his belief in God without even knowing it! It also was quite reassuring to see God's sense of humor at work. God was still loving his enemies and working in their lives to draw them closer to him.

I have a Jewish friend named Nathan. Nathan's father was from New York and had a Brooklyn accent. He pronounced Nathan's name Naten. Nathan's dad was a plumber and he taught Nathan the plumbing trade. Nathan told me that during the years he worked alongside his father they would frequently talk about God. After many of these discussions, his father would say, "Naten, thank God I'm an atheist!" They would both laugh and then continued on with the work at hand.

Nathan loved his dad and cherishes the time that they had together. Nathan doesn't hate anyone. He is the most cheerful guy that I have ever met in my life. Even though Nathan was diagnosed with terminal cancer and given six months to live, he still is as cheerful as ever. He loves people and helps the homeless in his community by giving clothes and food to them on a regular basis. It has been ten years since he was diagnosed with terminal cancer and God keeps giving Nathan the strength to carry on.

Love is wonderful The Beatles wrote: "All you need is love." That says it all doesn't it? And the Doobie Brothers wrote: "Where would you be without love?" The obvious answer to that question is - you would not be alive. If your parents didn't fall in love, we would not exist. We owe our very existence to love. We owe everything to love.

Most of us know that our parents love us. Even if they didn't exhibit the best parenting skills, they still love us. And in order to keep us safe and pointed in the right direction in life, our parents told us what to do and not to do. Nobody likes being told what to do, so sometimes we listened and sometimes we didn't. And through personal experiences we quickly learned that our parents were right. They told us things like: "Don't run into the street!" "Eat your vegetables." "Tell her you're sorry." "Don't hit your brother!" "Don't you dare take anything that doesn't belong to you!" "Don't you dare use that word in this house!" I could go on, but I think you get the picture.

Jesus makes it much simpler for us. He basically has two rules we should all follow. In

Matthew 22:37-40 Jesus says: "'Love the Lord God with all your heart, and all your soul and all your mind.' This is the first and greatest commandment. And the second is like it: 'Love your neighbor as yourself.' All the Law and Prophets hang on these two commandments." So, we are instructed to be in love with love and share that love with our neighbors.

In John 15:13 Jesus says: "Greater love has no one than this, that he lay down his life for his friends." Many people have sacrificed their lives for their friends. There have been many instances where soldiers have jumped on hand grenades to save their friends, or secret service officers taking a bullet for the people they were guarding. Well, Jesus Christ loves us so much, that he did the same thing. He laid down his life, so that we would be saved. Not in a physical sense, but in a spiritual sense.

Jesus came to earth to teach us how to live an abundant life. That life is found in Christ himself. Simply by asking Jesus into your own life, you are reborn spiritually. You become Christ's friend. And when it comes time for you to die, Christ will reach down to you and pull your spirit to heaven to be with him. He already did the dying for all of us. He laid down his life for his friends. And in the end, those who are friends of Jesus will be with him in heaven forever. This is every Christian's hope.

The Father, the Son and the Holy Spirit

In Genesis 1:26 God says: "Let us make man in our image, in our likeness, and let them rule over the fish of the sea and the birds of the air, over the livestock, over all the earth, and over all the creatures that move along the ground."

Please notice that it says: "Let us make man in our image..." God is speaking in the plural, using words like us and our instead of me and my. Who is with God when he said this? Jesus and the Holy Spirit were with God from the very beginning of man's creation. The "Holy Trinity" is in this great experiment together! And we, as human beings, are made in their image. So, we need only to look at ourselves to see a reflection of God, Jesus Christ and the Holy Spirit.

My father-in-law was a Christian, but he once told me that he couldn't understand the "Holy

Trinity". So, after a bit of thought, I asked him, "Are you a father?" And he said yes. Then I asked, "Aren't you also a son?" Again, he said yes. "And don't you have a spirit that lives within your body that gives it life?" The answer, of course, was yes. There you have it in a nutshell. The three are also representative of our mind, our body and our spirit. So, God is the brains behind this operation, Jesus is the body and the Holy Spirit is the energy that propels us and breathes life into us.

I am a building contractor and building a house offers a good physical representation of the "Holy Trinity". Building a home, like creating a human being, requires a collaborative effort. First you need an Architect. He is the brains of the operation. He designs the house, figures out how to orient the home on the site, decides on the window sizes and computes the required size of beams and nailing patterns used to build the structure. So, in this example, the architect is God. Then you need someone to build the structure. This person has to coordinate the purchasing and delivery of materials, the scheduling of workers and the supervising of the entire project from start to finish. This person represents Jesus, who in reality was a carpenter! The third requirement to build a house is energy. It not only takes electrical energy to run all the power tools, but it also takes human energy to haul the materials around, put them in place and complete the various tasks required to complete the structure. This energy represents the Holy Spirit.

When you stand inside a finished house, you can see the floor plan and the design features that the architect was responsible for. You can also see the materials that were chosen and the workmanship that went into the house. And you can imagine the energy that went into constructing it: The tools of the workers; the noise that was made; the dust and dirt and debris that was made; the communication that was needed to coordinate the building process; and finally, the blood, sweat and frustration of the workers who completed the project.

A house is also a representation of human beings. We also have a design to our bodies and materials that compose it and energy that drives it. Inside of us, there is a life that is lived just as there is a home life that is lived inside a home. There is noise going on constantly inside of us – thoughts. We make designs for our lives and think about how to carry out our plans. There is dirt and debris inside of us that we have to clean up and deal with; otherwise, it will accumulate and incapacitate us. There are a variety of emotions that live within us and pull us to act in one way or another. And of course, the most important thing that we need to have a happy life and a happy home life is love.

In Corinthians 13: 1-3 Saint Paul writes: "If I speak in the tongues of men and of angels, but have not love, I am only a resounding gong or a clanging cymbal. If I have the gift of prophecy and can fathom all mysteries and all knowledge, and if I have a faith that can move mountains, but have not love, I am nothing. If I give all I possess to the poor and surrender my body to the flames, but have not love, I gain nothing."

So, how do we get this love inside of us? We simply ask Jesus to forgive us for what we have done and ask him into our lives. So, no matter how badly we have behaved in the past, Jesus has the authority to forgive our sins. In Matthew 9:6 Jesus says, "But so that you may know that the son of man has authority on earth to forgive sins..." So

Jesus is the one who can help us lead a better life…a more abundant life. And remember, God, Jesus and the Holy Spirit love us and want to be part of our lives. Why not welcome them in? In Matthew 7:8 Jesus says, "For everyone who asks receives; he who seeks finds; and to him who knocks, the door will be opened."

Time to Party

Have you ever stood outside the door of a home where you had been invited to a party feeling a bit apprehensive about knocking on it? You start wondering if this party is going to be a dud. Will I have fun? Will I get along with the other people who have been invited? You finally get brave and knock on the door. The host answers and warmly welcomes you into their home. Instantly you are surrounded by lights and food and friendly people who begin engaging you in stimulating conversation. Soon you are filled with joy and tasty food and a feeling that you are special and loved and welcomed.

There's a story in the Bible about a son who asked his father for his share of his inheritance. The father, who loved his son, agreed and gave it to him. The son traveled to a far off place and lived high on the hog. He partied until his entire inheritance was gone. I am certain that he had a great time, even though he acted irresponsibly. Well, the next thing you know the son needed a job and all he could find was work on a pig farm. It was hard, dirty work and the living conditions and food he received were horrible. After working hard for a period of time, he realized that his life sucked!

He started thinking about how well his father treated the workers back home and he thought about returning home and going to work for him. He knew he blew it and was ashamed of what he had done. In spite of that, he still longed to be hack home. He was apprehensive about how he would be received. He told himself that he would apologize for his behavior and ask his father to forgive him and hire him as a laborer.

We pick up the story in Luke 15:20-24: "So he got up and went to his father. But while he was still a long way off, his father saw him and was filled with compassion for him; he ran to his son, threw his arms around him and kissed him

The son said to him, 'Father, I have sinned against heaven and against you. I am no longer worthy to be called your son.'

But the father said to his servants, 'Quick! Bring the best robe and put it on him. Put a ring on his finger and sandals on his feet. Bring the fattened calf and kill it. Let's have a feast and celebrate. For this son of mine was dead and is alive again, he was lost and is found! So they began to celebrate.

My favorite line from the movie "The Wizard of OZ" was spoken by Dorothy as she was clicking her ruby slippers together, "There's no place like home, there's no place like home."

Nearly all of us have made a home for ourselves.

It's a place where we are happy and comfortable to

be. It's someplace where we feel safe and secure.

Christians have a second home where they enjoy

returning to as well. It is called church and it

should be a warm welcoming place for people to

enter and be with others in God's family.

I'm a homebody. I love my physical home

and my church home and look forward to my

heavenly home as well. I love feeling snug and

warm and being around people who I love. I have

traveled to many places in the world but I must

agree with Dorothy – there's no place like home!

The parable above describes how God, our

father, is overjoyed whenever one of his lost

children returns to him. In Luke 15:7 Jesus says, "I

tell you that in the same way there will be more

rejoicing in heaven over one sinner who repents than over ninety-nine righteous persons, who do not need to repent."

As a sinner who has turned to Christ, I am glad to read that they are partying in heaven because of me! So, don't feel apprehensive about knocking on the door. Jesus will open it and welcome you into God's kingdom. Please, walk through the door and help keep the party in heaven going! You've heard the old saying, "The more, the merrier!"

The Father

Not all of us have biological fathers who are as compassionate as the father in the last chapter. Some fathers may leave their family or die. Others may be abusive to some degree. Others may have kicked their children out of their home! Many fathers are so busy with their own lives that they are simply not around much. Many fathers are indifferent. As a result, there are plenty of us who had a bad or non-existent relationship with our fathers.

My own father was physically and verbally abusive. Growing up I witnessed his brutality toward me, my mother and my three older brothers. He constantly complained about having to work, he drank considerable amounts of wine every evening and smoked three packs of cigarettes every day. As a result of his smoking habit, which he began when he was only nine years old, he died at the age of 49. He left my mother with nothing. Any time he had some extra money he either went out drinking or gambling. I was ten years old when he died.

Jesus has something to say about earthly father's who are not godly as well.

In John 8:44 Jesus says, "You belong to your father, the devil, and you want to carry out your father's desire. He was a murderer from the beginning, not holding to the truth, for there is no truth in him. When he lies, he speaks his native language, for he is a liar and the father of lies."

For many of us whose biological fathers may have hated God or became a victim of the devil's lies, it could be affecting our own lives as well. If you have ever felt that you and your siblings are still suffering from an abusive or destructive relationship with your father, it may be true. It is quite possible that you are being punished for the sins that your father had committed!

In Exodus 20:4-6 God is speaking directly to his people, "You shall not make for yourself an idol in the form of anything in heaven above or on the earth beneath or in the waters below. You shall not bow down to them or worship them; for I, the Lord your God, am a jealous God, punishing the children for the sin of the fathers to the third and fourth generation of those who hate me, but showing love to a thousand generations of those who love me and keep my commandments."

My siblings and I had been punished because of the sins of our father.

I had a horrible childhood but chose to accept Jesus and stop the punishment. One of my brothers was seriously injured in a plane crash at Pacoima Junior High in California. Another brother is suffering from HIV aids. Another brother was abusive to his wife and children. I am the only child in my family that has accepted Christ. It was a life changing event that has allowed me to live an abundant life.

In John 3:6-7 Jesus says, "Flesh gives birth to flesh, but the Spirit gives birth to spirit. You should not be surprised at my saying, 'You must be born again.'" So, our parents are responsible for our physical birth, but the Holy Spirit is responsible for our spiritual birth. And this is achieved by telling Jesus that you have screwed up and that you need Jesus to help you out. This must be an admission and request that is heart felt and sincere. Mere lip service will not fill you with the Holy Spirit and change your life!

In Mark 11:24 Jesus says, "Therefore I tell you, whatever you ask for in prayer, believe that you have received it, and it will be yours."

The good news is this: We have a heavenly father who loves us and wants us to be his children. In 2 Corinthians 6:18 it says, "I will be a father to you, and you will be my sons and daughters, says the Lord Almighty."

So how do we get to know "Our Father who art in heaven?" Once again we have to turn to Jesus. He is the closest representation of our heavenly Father. In John 10:27-30 Jesus says, "My sheep listen to my voice; I know them, and they follow me. I give them eternal life, and they shall never perish; no one can snatch them out of my hand. My Father, who has given them to me, is greater than all; no one can snatch them out of my Father's hand. I and the Father are one."

Imagine God in heaven holding the hand of Jesus on earth – "I and the Father are one," Jesus says. Now, imagine yourself grasping the other hand of Jesus – "...no one can snatch them out of my hand," says Jesus. And when the time comes, and our lives are over on earth, Jesus is still holding our hand. Not even death will snatch us away from his hand! He will pull our spirit up into heaven and we will grasp the hand of our heavenly Father. Jesus says, "...no one can snatch them out of my Father's hand.

Our heavenly Father loves us so much that he sent his own son down to earth to rescue us. In John 3:16-18 Jesus says, "For God so loved the world that he gave his one and only Son, that whoever believes in him shall not perish but have eternal life. For God did not send his Son into the world to condemn the world, but to save the world through him. Whoever believes in him is not condemned, but whoever does not believe stands condemned already because he has not believed in the name of God's one and only Son."

So please, grab the hand of Jesus. He will not let go of you. And no matter what happens in your life he will be with you always. Love never dies.

The Son

Have you ever wondered why Jesus was born into a poor blue collar family and ended up spending his first night on earth in an animal's food trough? It could be that God wanted his Son to experience the life that the common man lived at the time. He wanted Jesus to develop love and compassion for those in his community that were struggling to survive.

If you live or have lived in rural America, things are not all that different than they were in the time of Jesus. You have a small percentage of very wealthy land owners who live on land that was handed down to them and a few merchants in town that provide goods to the local population. The remainder provided labor and services to the community. Life is tough in rural America. People who live on small family farms are barely making it, unemployment is high and many people live on some form of government assistance. It's not a pretty picture now or 2,000 years ago.

Jesus worked right alongside others in the community as a carpenter. I'm sure Joseph, his earthly father, taught him the trade. In all likelihood, they had a great relationship and a strong bond. I'm sure Jesus was aware of many difficulties that others in his community were going through as he witnessed them first hand. Jesus was compelled to help those around him.

In the second chapter of Luke there are a few verses that give us an insight to Jesus as a boy: Luke 2:41-42 "Every year his parents went to Jerusalem for the Feast of the Passover. When he was twelve years old, they went up to the Feast, according to the custom." Jesus gets separated from his parents and they search for him. Luke 2:46-47

"After three days they found him in the temple courts, sitting among the teachers, listening to them and asking them questions. Everyone who heard him was amazed at his understanding and his answers." Luke 2:52 "And Jesus grew in wisdom and stature and in favor with God and men."

So, Jesus was a rather precocious child but he was also well accepted and appreciated. At the age of twelve he was already engaging in theological discussions with adults and as he matured, he became even wiser and more sought after by people in his community.

The Passover feast is still celebrated by Jews today. It is done in remembrance of what God had done in Egypt to help the Jews escape from slavery. The Egyptian ruler was refusing to let the Jews go free, so God told Moses to slaughter their lambs on the fourteenth day of the month and take the blood and smear some on the sides and tops of their doorframes.

In Exodus 12:12-13 God says, "On that same night I will pass through Egypt and strike down every firstborn – both men and animals – and I will bring judgment on all the gods of Egypt. I am the Lord. The blood will be a sign for you on the houses where you are; and when I see the blood, I will pass over you. No destructive plague will touch you when I strike Egypt."

Jesus is also known as the Lamb of God. In John 1:29 it says, "The next day, John saw Jesus coming toward him and said, 'Look, the Lamb of God, who takes away the sin of the world!'" So, Jesus is the new sacrificial lamb who gives up his life to take away the sin of the world. And it is through the blood of Jesus that Christians are saved. Those who ask Christ into their lives are "covered" by the sacrificial blood shed by Jesus when he was nailed to the cross. In the same way that the lamb's blood protected the Jews from God's plague in the book of Exodus, the blood of Jesus protects Christians from suffering an eternity in hell. When we, as Christians, die; God will see the blood of Christ on us and pass over us allowing Jesus to lift our spirits into heaven where we will live eternally. This is the hope of all Christians who have faith in Jesus.

The Holy Spirit

Jesus and our Heavenly Father speak to us through the Holy Spirit. And we speak to Jesus and God through the Holy Spirit as well. In today's society, the best analogy I can come up with is the internet. We speak to one another by E-mails, through the internet. However, if we don't have an internet connection we can't communicate. The Holy Spirit is like a high speed internet connection that allows us to have a personal conversation directly with Jesus and God.

This is a very real connection. Let me tell you a story. I remember commuting home from work in December several years ago. I was working for a Fortune 500 company headquartered in the Mid Wilshire district in Los Angeles. Normally, my commute back to Canoga Park in the San Fernando Valley took about an hour. However, for the past several days, it had been raining and that commute time stretched into two hours. So, on a Friday evening, after two weeks of two hour commutes, I'd had it!

There's got to be a better way home, I thought to myself. I flashed on a great idea. I would take Mulholland Road all the way to Topanga Canyon and miss all the horrible traffic. It was a great idea. I moved along nicely on Mulholland and made it into the Valley where the paved section of the road ended. Now, I had to make a decision. I either had to turn right and head down into and across the Valley on paved roads through stop and go traffic, or continue on the dirt portion of Mulholland to Topanga Canyon.

I had ridden down this dirt section several times on my motorcycle and I knew it was a long stretch of road with no other intersecting roads for miles. I drove onto the dirt road for a bit just to test how firm the roadbed was. I got out of my car and looked ahead as far as I could see, which wasn't very far, and decided it looked solid enough to drive on. I was doing great and estimated that I was about half way to Topanga Canyon when suddenly the road turned to soft mud.

I was driving a Chevy Vega at the time. This car had very little ground clearance, and I could hear the mud hitting the under carriage of the car. Swell, I thought to myself. I am literally in the middle of nowhere here! So, I decided to keep on going. The car tires were kicking up so much mud onto my windshield that my wiper blades could not keep the glass clean I had to roll down my window and use my hand to clear a small porthole to peek through.

There I was, in a car that was fish tailing all over the road, driving with one hand on the wheel and another hand frantically wiping a small patch of windshield clean. I can do this, I kept telling myself. After a mile or two I saw a car up ahead that was stuck at the base of a long steep hill. The red car was stopped diagonally in the road. I looked to my right and saw that there was a steep drop off . What now, I wondered?

If I stopped, that would be the end of it. I would suffer the same fate as the driver in the red car. It was starting to get dark. I eased the car to the right as I approached the stuck car. With luck, I could make it. I narrowly missed the stranded vehicle as I passed it only to confront a slippery uphill grade. Steady on the accelerator, I thought to myself. I was doing well, but near the top of the hill my car started to lug in second gear. I knew that the car would die if I didn't downshift, but I also knew that downshifting would break my momentum and risk spinning my wheels as I released the clutch.

It was a lose-lose situation. I downshifted, the wheels spun, the car turned sideways and plop! My rear wheels went off the road and sunk into some very soft muck. As I stepped out of the car, my foot sank knee deep into the mud. I thought that I might be able to jack up the rear end of the car and shove some bushes under the rear tires to gain some traction. As I started to pump the jack handle, I watched in horror as the base of the jack was sinking into the mud with each push of the jack handle.

Great! It was nearly dark now and raining. I was standing knee deep in mud wearing my new three piece suit wondering what the solution to my problem was. Oh Lord, I thought. I bowed my head and said, I need a four wheel drive vehicle with a winch to drive down the road and pull me out of this mess. When I opened my eyes and looked up the road, I saw a set of headlights! Could it be? I heard the throaty exhaust of a V-8 engine as the vehicle slowly made its way down the road to where I was standing.

As it drove around the last bend in the road, before reaching me, I could hardly believe my eyes. There it was, a Jeep with a winch on the front of it! The driver got out of his vehicle, hooked me up to his winch and pulled me out of my predicament.

I gave him whatever cash I had in my pocket and drove home the rest of the way without any more trouble.

In Matthew 6:7-8 Jesus says, "And when you pray, do not keep on babbling like pagans, for they think they will be heard because of their many words. Do not be like them, for your Father knows what you need before you ask him." So, God knew exactly what I needed on that mountainside long before I was even stuck. His loving kindness set in motion the events that rescued me on that cold, rainy December evening.

So, you might ask, how do you sign up for this "internet service" called the Holy Spirit? John the Baptist, a prophet who baptizes Jesus, says in Matthew 3:11, "I baptize you with water for repentance. But after me will come one who is more powerful than I, whose sandals I am not fit to carry. He will baptize you with the Holy Spirit and with fire." Once again, Jesus is the ticket to ride! Accepting Jesus into your life will hook you up to the Holy Spirit.

In John 16:13 Jesus says, "But when he, the Spirit of truth comes, he will guide you into all truth. He will not speak on his own; he will speak only what he hears, and he will tell you what is yet to come." This verse reminds me of another interesting story. I was camping with some friends at the beach on the central California coast. I had a wonderful dinner consisting of a can of tuna washed down with some red wine and a bunch of Oreo cookies for desert.

There were four of us camping that night. A full moon rose and cast enough light for us to hike along the beach. We walked for awhile and then saw a path that went up a cliff that overlooked the ocean. The moon provided just enough light for us to see. There was a broad, flat field at the top with dried grass that was nearly knee high. We all looked out at the ocean of black ink with slivers of moonlight shimmering on the surface. It was a stunning view. A couple of the guys started horsing around and wrestling each other.

After returning to camp, I crawled into my sleeping bag and was about to fall asleep when my friend, Randy, said that he had lost his wallet up on the grassy field where he had been wrestling. Before I knew it, the Holy Spirit got a hold of me and spoke these words through me, "Don't worry Randy. I'll find your wallet." I put on my pants and shoes and headed back to the beach. I simply let go of myself and let the Holy Spirit guide me along the beach, up the cliff face and into the grassy field. I walked a way into the field and my body stopped. I heard the Holy Spirit tell me to bend down and reach out my hand. I slowly bent over and reached down into the tall weeds and my hand fell upon a leather wallet!

In Matthew 19:26 Jesus says, "With man this is impossible, but with God all things are possible." It was a remarkable experience that I will never forget. The Holy Spirit told Randy, through me, that I would find his wallet, and he led me right to it! How can you not trust in something so mind boggling? If the four of us searched the entire night, we probably could not have found Randy's wallet. But with God, all things are possible.

Miracles

Harry Bosch, a character in several Michael Connelly detective novels, has stated repeatedly that there are no coincidences. I agree. Have you ever experienced truly bizarre coincidences in your life? Something that happened to you that made you step back and think – I wonder what the odds were of that happening? Or perhaps you walked away from a horrible accident or situation without serious injury or death? Then you have experienced a miracle!

In Psalm 77:14 it says, "You are the God who performs miracles; you display your power among the peoples." In other words, God reveals himself to us through miracles. I have shared a couple miracles in my life with you. Think back on your own personal experience. Have you ever walked away from a situation thinking that you were extraordinarily lucky? Perhaps God was revealing himself to you.

In the spring of 1975, I was in Cartagena, Colombia. I had spent the past six months traveling through Mexico, Central America, Ecuador and Colombia. I had already purchased an airline ticket to Miami, Florida and was carrying it with me in my pocket. It was morning and I was heading to the central market to buy a smoothie from my favorite vendor. I was about a block away when a small army troop carrier came screeching to a halt right in front of me.

I was accustomed to seeing the military in several countries in Latin America. They frequently traveled on trains and buses to insure the safety of passengers from guerilla insurgents. Within seconds ten soldiers surrounded me with their M16's drawn and pointed at me. They started yelling and motioning to me to get into their truck. The Holy Spirit spoke to me and told me, whatever you do, don't go into that truck!

I slowly put out my hand and told them to calm down and that I had my papers. As I slowly moved my hand to my pocket to retrieve my passport, I began speaking Spanish to them. I told them how much I loved their country and language and met many good people during my stay in Colombia. I held my passport out to the group and the commander came over and grabbed it from me. His initial angry look started to soften as I continued talking to them.

Explaining to them that this was my last day in their country, I slowly reached back into my pocket for my plane ticket. I told them that this was my plane ticket to Miami, Florida and that I was leaving tomorrow morning. I handed the ticket to the commander as I looked him right in the eye and could tell that he was becoming uncertain and guilty about his actions.

By this time, all the soldiers had their assault rifles at their side and they were smiling at me. Finally, the commander handed me back my passport and plane ticket and motioned me to continue on my way. I wished them all a great day and told them it was a pleasure to visit with them. The Holy Spirit was guiding me through the entire exchange with the soldiers. I was not the least bit afraid because I felt the presence of God and had faith that I would be protected.

In Psalm 32:7 it says, "You are my hiding place, you will protect me from trouble and surround me with songs of deliverance." Our heavenly father is with us and cares enough about us to protect us through miracles.

The most incredible spiritual event that had occurred to me happened in August of 1990. My wife and I were living in Sacramento, California and we had just purchased a ranch in Scott Valley, California. Our house was on the market and I was commuting back and forth to the ranch where I was adding about 800 square feet of living space to a run down two bedroom one bath farm house on our property. It was a Saturday night and I was in Sacramento lying in bed wondering if we were doing the right thing. Slowly, I began feeling the presence of Jesus in the room. In my minds eye, I could see him there with me. I became filled with an incredible peace and euphoria that I have never experienced in my entire life! Jesus was right there with me in my room!

After blessing me with his presence, his being began to depart. I wanted to go with him. I clung to his spirit and was unwilling to break this phenomenal connection. Jesus knew it was not my time to leave with him. I felt his power growing and expanding until BOOM, a transformer in our back yard blew up and our lights went out. The frightening noise broke our connection and punctuated a spiritual experience with a real life event.

In Matthew 5:8 Jesus says, "Blessed are the pure in heart for they will see God."

About a year later, I was standing out in our pasture getting ready to turn off our irrigation system. It was a warm summer evening and there was just enough light left to do this last chore before calling it a day. As I stood out in the field, I began asking God to show me a sign. I told him that I was unsure whether this was where he wanted me to be. I pleaded with and asked him to please show me a sign so that I can know that I am doing the right thing.

Slowly, the sky started to become lighter. At first I thought that maybe a car with bright headlights was heading up our road, but there was no car to be seen or heard. It just continued growing lighter and lighter until our entire field was as bright as day! I saw a small, brilliant white light hanging over our home. The small sphere of light grew larger and larger then suddenly burst into an incredible cloud of luminescent green that expanded until it filled half the evening sky. In an instant, it disappeared.

I was concerned about my wife and kids who were at home. I jumped into our station wagon and flew over the dirt road that led back home. Pulling into our driveway, I frantically slammed on the brakes and rushed inside. My wife was very calmly sitting on our sofa with our children reading a bedtime story to them. I started shouting, "Did you see that? Did you see what just happened?" My wife quietly told me that yes they had seen the bright light. I was so thankful that they were all fine. "Wow," was all I could say.

In John 20:30-31 it says, "Jesus did many other miraculous signs in the presence of his disciples, which are not recorded in this book. But these are written that you may believe that Jesus is the Christ, the son of God, and that by believing you may have life in his name."

What is The Truth?

Everyone wants to know the truth. Why is that? In Psalm 51:6 it says, "Surely you desire truth in the inner parts;" So, there is something deep inside of us that needs to know the truth. At one point in time, everyone believed that the world was flat and that the sun revolved around the earth. Today, we no longer believe that. Back in the 1960's when I was in high school; I was taught that atoms consisted of protons, neutrons and electrons. Today we know that atoms are far more complex than that.

So, what once was "believed" to be true, was in reality a lie. If someone spoke the truth during the time that it was "believed" that the world was flat, they would have been branded a lunatic and possibly even killed. The truth cannot be transitory. Something is either true, or it is not. In

John 8:45 Jesus says, "Yet because I tell the truth, you do not believe me!" How can we know the truth?

Many people choose to believe President Obama is a Muslim and not an American citizen. The truth is, he is a Christian and an American citizen. So, something can be true even though some people refuse to believe it. The converse of that is also true: Something can be false and some people believe it. So, when seeking the truth, it seems that our beliefs sometimes get in the way of the truth. Whether you choose to believe the truth or not, is up to you. However, an absolute truth does exist and we all yearn to know the truth.

Here is a spiritual truth: Darkness and light cannot coexist in the same space. So if you walk into a dark room and turn on the light, the darkness will flee and everything will be bathed in light. In

John 8:12 Jesus says, "I am the light of the world. Whoever follows me will never walk in darkness, but will have the light of life." So if your internal life is filled with darkness, depression, fear etc., just ask Jesus in and the darkness will flee. Your life will brighten up in no time!

Sometimes, people can be very stubborn and prideful. They may know that their lives are a mess and that they are living in darkness. No matter what you tell them, they will not believe the truth. In Matthew 7:6 Jesus says, "Do not give dogs what is sacred; do not throw your pearls to pigs." The ultimate destiny of these poor people is found in 2 Thessalonians 2:10: "They perish because they refused to love the truth and so be saved."

So how can you tell who is being truthful? In Matthew 7:16-18 Jesus says, "By their fruit you will recognize them. Do people pick grapes from thornbushes or figs from thistles? Likewise every good tree bears good fruit, but a bad tree bears bad fruit." So, by observing a person's life, you should be able to discern weather they are living in truth or not. Does their life have order? Are they polite and respectful? Are they compassionate, gracious and hard working? Are they considerate? Do they listen to you and are they concerned about your welfare? Well, chances are, they are living in truth. On the other hand, are they the sort of person who lies, cheats, and has no respect or self discipline? Are their lives constantly in a mess? Do they have questionable morals and always wondering what's in it for them? Sounds like bad fruit to me!

In John 3:20-21 Jesus says, "Everyone who does evil hates the light, and will not come into the light for fear that his deeds will be exposed. But whoever lives by the truth comes into the light, so that it may be seen plainly that what he has done has been done through God." Many people do not want to believe that there is absolute truth. They do not want to commit to accepting this concept. Why? Because they want to delude themselves into believing that there are "gray" areas. They want to obscure the truth.

In John 8:31-32 Jesus says, "...If you hold to my teaching, you are really my disciples. Then you will know the truth, and the truth will set you free." In other words, if you believe in Jesus, lay down all your hurt, your guilt and your shame before Him, he will release those burdens from you and set you free. You will be uplifted and free to experience life as it should be.

Another spiritual truth is this: There is both good and evil in the world. Jesus is the most shining example of good and the devil is the darkest example of evil. In Ephesians 6:12 it says, "For our struggle is not against flesh and blood, but against the rulers, against the authorities, against the powers of this dark world and against the spiritual forces of evil in the heavenly realms." In other words, our battle in life is against evil – both in this world and the spiritual world.

We are not fighting people, or flesh and blood, we are fighting evil. The evil we are fighting may be inside of a human being and it may have completely taken over that person. Or, it could be the evil that is in the spiritual world. This "ethereal" evil could be a little thought placed in our minds suggesting that we do something harmful to ourselves or others. It could be a nightmare that haunts us or it could be a feeling of an evil presence in our room when we wake up in the middle of the night.

In Mark 5:2-8 it says, "When Jesus got out of the boat, a man with an evil spirit came from the tombs to meet him. This man lived in the tombs, and no one could bind him any more, not even with a chain. For he had often been chained hand and foot, but he tore the chains apart and broke the irons on his feet. No one was strong enough to subdue him. Night and day among the tombs and in the hills he would cry out and cut himself with stones.

When he saw Jesus from a distance, he ran and fell on his knees in front of him. He shouted at the top of his voice, 'What do you want with me Jesus, Son of the Most High God? Swear to God that you won't torture me.' For Jesus had said to him, 'Come out of this man, you evil spirit.'" After the evil spirit left the man, he was extremely grateful. In Mark 5:18-20 it says, "As Jesus was getting into the boat, the man who had been demon possessed begged to go with him. Jesus did not let him, but said, 'Go home to your family and tell them how much the Lord has done for you, and how he has had mercy on you."

Jesus did not harm the man who was possessed. But he fought the evil within the man and commanded the evil to leave. How can we fight evil in our own lives when we are confronted by it? In James 4:7-8 it says, "Submit yourselves, then, to God. Resist the devil, and he will flee from you. Come near to God and he will come near to you..." James tells us to resist the devil. Just say "no" to the devil's schemes. That's a no brainer. But how do you come near to God? Accepting Christ into your life is the first step. The next step is praying the prayer that Jesus teaches us in Matthew 6:9-13:

"This, then, is how you should pray:

'Our Father in heaven,

hallowed be your name,

your kingdom come,

your will be done

    on earth as it is in heaven.

Give us today our daily

    bread.

Forgive us our debts,

    as we also have forgiven

        our debtors.

And lead us not into

    temptation,

but deliver us from the evil one.'"

I pray this prayer often. I pray it when I wake up in the morning and when I go to bed at night. If something freaks me out like a nightmare, or the presence of an evil force, or something I just can't handle, I recite this prayer. I recite a little different version of it, as it was taught to me by Catholic sisters - to whom I am greatly indebted. This is the way that I come near to God, and in return, God comes near to me.

Prayer

Staying in touch with your friends and family is important. Getting together for special events keeps us connected with one another. *"Facebook"* helps us all keep in touch with one another as well. Social networks, whether on line or not, are important to our well being. We are social creatures and we need others in our lives to care for us, talk to us and laugh with us. It is these relationships that help us get by in life. My best relationships in life are with my heavenly Father, Jesus and the Holy Spirit. They are a big part of my social network and I regularly stay in touch with them through prayer.

So what is prayer? Prayer is simply a conversation with our heavenly Father and Jesus, spoken through the Holy Spirit. Sometimes we all have sensitive issues that we need to talk about and resolve. Perhaps we may be too embarrassed or ashamed to talk about them with our family or friends. Well, God and Jesus are always available to listen to you no matter where or when. They are also extremely good at helping you resolve touchy issues or helping you out of a bad situation.

They are good at it because they love you, care for you and value you. .In Matthew 6:25-27 Jesus says, "Therefore I tell you, do not worry about your life, what you will eat or drink, or about your body, what you will wear. Is not life more important than food, and the body more important than clothes? Look at the birds of the air; they do not sow or reap or store away in barns, and yet your heavenly Father feeds them. Are you not much more valuable than they? Who of you by worrying can add a single hour to his life?" So, if there are issues that are troubling you, talk to your heavenly

Father and Jesus. Unload those burdens onto them and ask them for their help. You might just be surprised at the outcome.

Prayer is a powerful tool. I can't tell you how many times that my prayers have been answered. Prayers for healing, strength, wisdom, safety, work, direction, and courage have all been answered. Some of my prayers were answered quickly and others took years. But throughout my life, God has been faithful. In Psalm 33: 4 it says, "For the word of the Lord is right and true, he is faithful in all he does." Prayers don't have to be formal and wordy. The shortest prayer that I have ever heard was uttered by a minister just before his sermon. It went like this: "Dear heavenly Father. Help! In Jesus name, amen." It was a bit shocking but heartfelt and honest.

Life today is far more complicated and fast moving than it once was. As a result, more and more people need help. In Matthew 7:7-8 Jesus says, "Ask and it will be given to you; seek and you will find; knock and the door will be opened to you. For everyone who asks receives, he who seeks finds; and to him who knocks, the door will be opened." Just for fun, watch a movie that was filmed before 1950. The scenes are much longer and there are far fewer cuts made than current films. Don't get me wrong, some of these older films are great but they do move rather slowly. They reflect a slower pace of life that is long gone.

The heightened pace of life has a huge byproduct: Stress. With cell phones, laptops, smart phones and iPods, we have fewer moments when we can just stop, take a deep breath and enjoy our surroundings. While these devices help keep us connected and entertained, they can also rob us of opportunities to interact with others. I like to keep in shape, so I have been going to our local gym for the past ten years. I used to enjoy chatting with people while working out or in between sets. Since the introduction of the iPod, there have been more and more people showing up at the gym with ear buds plugged in listening to their favorite tunes. The problem is, I can't interact with them. The signal that they are sending out is: Don't talk to me. So, even though we have all these devices to help us stay connected and entertained, we are missing out on new opportunities to expand our social network and develop deeper relationships with those around us.

We all yearn for great relationships. Relationships make life sweet and help reduce stress. The more close friends we have, the more we can talk about the difficulties we are experiencing in life. And in return, we can listen to our friends and mull over their advice. When our friends call, we recognize their voice immediately and just hearing their voice brightens us up. In John 10:27 Jesus says, "My sheep listen to my voice, I know them and they follow me." So, if you need to talk to a friend and listen to their advice give Jesus a call.

Faith

What is faith? It is an unquestioning belief that does not require proof or evidence. So, faith is a deep belief. We all have faith in something. I have faith in gravity. You don't have to show me proof or evidence that gravity exists. After nearly 60 years of experience, I can honestly say that I believe in gravity. I also have faith that the investments I have made in the stock market will be worth more in the future than they are worth today. If I didn't have that belief, I wouldn't be investing in the stock market.

Faith, in today's world, takes a back seat to science. I can't tell you how many times I have heard someone say to someone else, "Prove it!" This demand is like the throwing down of the gauntlet in medieval times when one knight challenges the other to a fight. The shouting of "prove it" usually ends the argument. How do you "prove" something? If you accuse someone of lying, how can you prove it? If someone is lying, and believes in the lie, there is no way you are going to change that person's mind. So, why bother trying to prove it?

Jesus was confronted by a similar situation in the New Testament. In Matthew 16:1 it says, "The Pharisees and Sadducees came to Jesus and tested him by asking him to show them a sign from heaven." In other words, these ruling elites were asking Jesus to "prove it". They wanted him to "prove" that he was the Son of God. A similar situation today would be having a Congressional committee asking Jesus to prove that he was the Son of God. Jesus merely chose to walk away from the challenge. He knew, no matter what he did, that these individuals had already made up their minds about him.

In Matthew 17:20 Jesus says, "...I tell you the truth, if you have faith as small as a mustard seed, you can say to the mountain, 'Move from here to there' and it will move. Nothing will be impossible for you." Obviously, my faith is smaller than a mustard seed. But, the point that Jesus was making is this: If you want to do something great in life, you are going to need faith. Having faith is not easy when you are being barraged by choruses of "prove it" throughout your life. Even Peter, one of the disciples of Jesus, did not have the strength to defend his faith in Christ after Jesus was arrested. In Matthew 26:34 Jesus says to Peter, "I tell you the truth," Jesus answered, "this very night, before the rooster crows, you will disown me three times." And Peter did just as Jesus predicted.

If you have faith in Jesus, you will have the strength to accomplish things in life that you would not be able to do otherwise. But, like Peter, even those of us who do have faith in Jesus have difficulty upholding that faith. Our faith is constantly being tested by our own culture as well as the "spiritual forces of evil" that Paul talks about in Ephesians 6:12. Our faith in Jesus is the foundation that provides us the strength to have faith in ourselves and what we are doing and how we are living. In Matthew 7:24-25 Jesus says, "Therefore everyone who hears these words of mine and puts them into practice is like a wise man who built his house on the rock. The rain came down, the streams rose, and the winds blew and beat against the house, yet it did not fail, because it had its foundation on the rock."

So, our faith in Jesus is the foundation on which we build our life. But Jesus warns us to set that foundation on "the rock" so that the struggles that we all face in life do not undermine our faith in Christ. So, in this analogy what is "the rock"? That question is answered in Psalm 18:2 where it says, "The Lord is my rock, my fortress and my deliverer; my God is my rock in whom I take refuge. He is my shield and the horn of my salvation, my stronghold." Strength is found in unity. Ask any general, sports team, or political party and I am sure they would agree. So, if you build your house, which is symbolic of your life, on a solid foundation, which is Jesus, and set that foundation on the rock, which is God, you will have a great life!

Get a Life

I once heard someone on TV say, "He who dies with the most toys wins." This statement really bothered me, and I could never forget it. What kind of life, I wondered, would a person who believes this statement have? When I was in my mid twenties, I thought that buying a new car would make my life great! I was so excited when I purchased my new Chevy Vega. This was really going to be it. After driving it off the lot, I felt proud. I kept it cleaned and polished, showed it off to my friends and family members but do you know what? It didn't change my life. I had my same old life in a new car. It was a good life lesson for me. New possessions, no matter how many of them you purchase, will not change your life in a meaningful way.

A person who spends his entire life obsessed with acquiring things has no life. He or she has things, but no life. In Luke 12:15 Jesus says, "...watch out! Be on your guard against all kinds of greed; a man's life does not consist in the abundance of his possessions." We all have priorities in life, but accumulating "toys" should not be one of them. So then, what should our priorities in life be? I can tell you what mine are. My first priority is Jesus. I tried living without Jesus for the first 21 years of my life, and I can tell you with assurance that it wasn't pretty. So, Jesus is my number one priority and my "go to guy". If I have a problem, I go to Jesus and ask him for help. In John 10:10 Jesus says, "...I have come that they may have life, and have it to the full."

My second priority in life is my family. In Ephesians 5:25 it says, "Husbands, love your wives, just as Christ loved the church and gave himself up for her..." So, we as husbands are basically instructed to take a bullet for our wives if need be. In John 15:13 Jesus says, "Greater love has no one than this, that he lay down his life for his friends." My wife and children are my best friends. I would like to think, that if it became necessary to do so, that I would lay down my life for them. My life is secondary to that of my family. I take care of their needs before considering my own needs. As any good parents do, my wife and I have made many sacrifices to help our children.

Work is my next priority. In Colossians 3:23 it says, "Whatever you do, work at it with all your heart, as working for the Lord, not for men..." Work is important, but it should not be your first priority in life. We have learned that love should be our first priority – love for God and love for our neighbor. So, if you are putting work first in your life, chances are that you are more interested in money than love. In Matthew 6:24 Jesus says, "No one can serve two masters. Either he will hate the one and love the other, or he will be devoted to the one and despise the other. You cannot serve both God and money."

This reminds me of an old Beatle song: "Can't Buy Me Love" The following lines form the refrain in the song and they are sung several times:

"Cause I don't care too much for money

For money can't buy me love"

Love is something that is given or received for free. You can't buy it, and so it is stated in the song's title. It's a great song and a great thing to remember and make a part of your life. We receive God's love for free and we can freely love God in return. It's a wonderful loving relationship that is absolutely free. You can't buy God's love and you can't earn God's love. It is freely given. All you have to do, is freely receive it.

Many of you have been in one sided relationships where someone else expressed their love for you but, for whatever reason, you felt uncomfortable accepting that love. You may have walked away from that relationship. Years later, you may have regretted doing that. With God, there are no regrets. God is always there and always loves you. All you need to do is be willing to open the door to that love and receive it. Jesus says, in Rev 3:20, "Here I am! I stand at the door and knock. If anyone hears my voice and opens the door, I will come in and eat with him, and he with me."

I was born into a poor immigrant family. My three older brothers were all born overseas. As

I was growing up, I felt disadvantaged and I didn't like it. When I became a young man I was determined to become a millionaire. My wife and I both worked hard. I started a real estate company in Sacramento and she worked for the State of California. In the first ten years of our married life, we turned $10,000 into $750,000. As I was approaching my goal of becoming a millionaire, I began to think: What happens once I achieve my goal? What then? Do I change my goal to become a multi-millionaire? That seemed very shallow to me. In Ecclesiastes 5:10 it says, "Whoever has money never has money enough; whoever loves wealth is never satisfied with his income. This too is meaningless."

All my life, I have viewed money as a tool. It was a tool that I could use to purchase life's essentials and something else that I have always valued highly – time. If I had some extra money, I could take some time off and spend it with my family or use it to pursue other interests, like writing for instance. My wife and I used the money we had accumulated to help finance the six years we lived in the country. This was a special time for all of us. We all experienced a great deal of personal and spiritual growth during those years. We built precious memories that will last us a lifetime.

Money is a tool. Why would anyone be in love with a tool? Currently, I am a building contractor. I own and use many tools in my line of work. I can't say that I have a favorite tool, but if I were to choose a tool that is most useful to me, it would be a hammer. I carry two hammers in my tool belt at all times. One is a framing hammer that I use for slamming in large nails and also for demolition work. It has a waffle pattern on its head that provides good traction on nail heads. On the opposite end is a claw that I use for pulling out nails, prying boards apart and sometimes digging in the dirt. My other hammer is a finish hammer; it has a smooth face and claw on the other end as well. Although each hammer is quite useful, I can honestly say that I do not love my hammers.

People get into trouble when they cross over the threshold of using money as a tool, to loving money. In 1st Timothy 6:9-10 it says, "People who want to get rich fall into temptation and a trap and into many foolish and harmful desires that plunge men into ruin and destruction. For the love of money is a root of all kinds of evil." Many of us are facing the destructive power of this "love of money" that led to the financial melt down of 2008. Every person who owns stock or owns a home in the United States took a big hit on their investments as a result of the near collapse of our financial system. All of this resulted from pure unadulterated greed! For those of you who have fallen into this greed mentality please take note of what it says in 1st Timothy 6:7: "For we brought nothing into the world, and we can take nothing out of it."

Children

The most fun that I have ever had in my life was raising our four children with my wife. It was quite a bit of work and took a great deal of patience, but it was entirely worth it. We have a great relationship with all our children and I believe that they are our living legacy. We may not be able to take anything out of this world when we die but we feel comfort knowing that we brought love into the world through the lives of our children.

When my first son came home from the hospital, I realized that I did not have a clue about being a father. Quickly, my wife and I discovered that he only cried for three reasons. He was either hungry, needed a diaper change or simply wanted to be held. This reduced the stress factor tremendously. It is amazing how quickly I bonded to this little child. Having a child also made me appreciate and value other children and other parents. Becoming a father turned me into a much better person in general. It also made me realize that I really love little children.

Jesus loved little children as well. In Matthew 19:14 Jesus says, "...Let the little children come to me, and do not hinder them, for the kingdom of heaven belongs to such as these." So, why does the kingdom of heaven belong to "such as these"? Let's look at the characteristics of young children. They are trusting, loving, honest, innocent and direct. How can you not like little children? The real question is: What happened to us along the way to adulthood?

Bad stuff happens to all of us and no parents are absolutely perfect. As a result, we can lose some of the pureness of the wonderful traits that children possess. As we mature, many of us have been hurt by a friend or family member and we have become less loving than we once were. Words were spoken or actions were taken that changed our relationship with someone and made us more reluctant to love people as easily as we once did. Perhaps someone bullied us as children and made us more unwilling to trust other people. Some of us may have experienced harsh acts committed against us and stripped us of our childhood innocence. Perhaps we told someone how we really felt about them and were punished for it resulting in our inability to be frank with people. Possibly the people in our lives were dishonest and we grew up believing that this was normal human behavior.

As a result of our negative life experiences, we all have scars, both physical and psychological. In Matthew 18:3 Jesus says, "…I tell you the truth, unless you change and become like little children, you will never enter the kingdom of heaven." So, we need to figure out a way to become like little children again. We need to regain those attributes of trust, love, honesty, innocence and directness. In other words, we need to get in touch with our "inner child".

Dealing with all the accumulated hurt in our lives takes time. The first step is to acknowledge to ourselves that we do indeed have baggage that we are carting around that weighs us down. As we think of individuals and situations that have caused us pain in the past, we need to allow them to surface and deal with them. We need to forgive others for the hurt that they have caused us. We need to tell ourselves that this suitcase is just too darn heavy to keep dragging around with us. We need to unpack this sucker and make life easier for us and those around us.

Everyone knows that unpacking a suitcase is no fun. But, it has to be done. It would be nice if we could just chuck the whole piece of luggage at once! Unfortunately, unpacking our psychological baggage takes time and persistence. Some items in our bag may reappear. Just keep tossing them out until they no longer return. Sometimes you might pull things out and realize that you were the one that caused hurt to someone else. In these situations, you need to ask God to forgive you for what you have done and then yank that thing out of your suitcase. Believe me, the stuff in your baggage is old and out of style and is of no use to anyone.

Have you ever gone through your closet and pulled out stuff that you never wear? You either throw it away or take it to the Goodwill. Don't you feel better afterwards? You don't have to keep looking at stuff you don't wear anymore. You no longer have to keep moving clothes around that you never pull off of hangers. And, the big bonus is, you have room to hang up new clothes! Eliminating your psychological baggage should have the same effect. It will free up your emotions and make you feel better about yourself. And, it will free up space for new people and new experiences.

In the traditional "Lord's Prayer" it says, "Forgive us our trespasses, as we forgive those who trespass against us." In order to become more like little children, we all need to forgive others for what they have done to us, and ask God to forgive us for what we have done to others. In Mark 9:37 Jesus says, "Whoever welcomes one of these little children in my name welcomes me…" To become more like a little child is to become more like Jesus.

Judging

It's easy to be a critic. We all have opinions about every aspect of life. We all talk about and criticize people, clothes, restaurants, performances, movies, vacation spots… It's nearly an endless list isn't it? Let's take a deeper look into what it takes to be a critic. In order to make criticisms you first have to judge what you are criticizing. In order to "judge" you need to observe and analyze. Every minute detail must be examined and conclusions must be made.

How many times have you heard someone ask, "On a scale of 1 to 10 with one being the worst and 10 being the best how does this rate?" We are constantly weighing and measuring everything in life. Judging seems to come naturally to all of us. Don't get me wrong, some things are important to judge to insure our survival. Is the meat in the refrigerator spoiled? Is this situation safe? Is this person trying to con me?

We need to make judgments at work as well. Which investment would be better to make? How can I make this more efficient? Where can I cut costs? I am a building contractor and one of the most obvious areas in which I need to make judgments is when I am purchasing lumber. When I go to Home Depot, I push my oversized shopping cart over to the bins that hold boards. I pick up each piece, bring it up to my eye and check to see if it is twisted or excessively bowed. If it is, I throw it to the back of the pile and pick up another board. I continue doing this until I have all the boards that are on my shopping list.

In Matthew 7:3-5 Jesus says, "Why do you look at the speck of sawdust in your brother's eye and pay no attention to the plank in your own eye?

How can you say to your brother, 'Let me take the speck out of your eye,' when all the time there is a plank in your own eye? You hypocrite, first take the plank out of your own eye, and then you will see clearly to remove the speck from your brother's eye." We are all too preoccupied judging others. As we size people up, we notice the minutest imperfections such as a speck in someone's eye and we are quick to point out these defects. It is much easier for us to be critical of others than it is for us to admit our own shortcomings. We need to remove the board from our eye and stop being so judgmental. If we look at people with more compassion and understanding and develop a more humble attitude, we will have much better relationships with others.

Have you ever been out in public somewhere and noticed someone checking you out?

Doesn't it bother you? It probably makes you think: "How dare he stand there and judge me; he doesn't even know me!" In Galatians 2:6 it says, "...God does not judge by external appearance..." If God does not judge by external appearance, perhaps we shouldn't either. In Matthew 7:1-2 Jesus says, "Do not judge, or you too will be judged, and with the measure you use, it will be measured to you." So the more critical you are of others, the more critical they will be of you. This is definitely a "lose-lose" situation.

Thankfully, Jesus did not come to earth to judge us. He came to teach us how to have a better life, free us from the grasp of evil and give us the opportunity to have everlasting life in heaven. In John 12:47 Jesus says, "...For I did not come to judge the world, but to save it." Thank God for that!

Anger

Do you have to commute to work? If you do, the chances are that you get angry at least once during the day. You might get angry because traffic is moving slower than usual and making you late for work. Another driver might cut you off, or swerve into your lane or be driving three inches from your rear bumper making your face turn red with road rage. Or someone may have forgotten to put gas in their car and they are now blocking your lane. There are multiple opportunities to get angry during a single day!

Anger is a byproduct of judging. While you are driving your car you are judging the drivers around you and if you determine that someone is driving poorly, you get angry. If you are at a restaurant and you judge that the waiter is taking too long to serve you or the chef overcooks your steak, you get angry. If you pay for a performance that you judge was not worth watching, you get angry.

When you do get angry, it is important to maintain your composure and not do anything stupid. In Proverbs 29:11 it says, "A fool gives full vent to his anger, but a wise man keeps himself under control." If you over react and hit someone or cause an accident or kill someone, you may end up spending a long time in prison as a result of your unchecked anger. In Deuteronomy 32:35 God says, "It is mine to avenge; I will repay." Letting God repay someone for the injustice that they have caused you is a much smarter way to deal with anger. After all, no one is going to arrest God for punishing a perpetrator.

Becoming less judgmental will help you become less angry. After all, we all make mistakes

– including driving errors. The Bible suggests that we try to stay away from people who have "anger management" issues. In Proverbs 22:24-25 it says, "Do not make friends with a hot-tempered man, do not associate with one easily angered, or you may learn his ways and get yourself ensnared." It's best to tone down our judgment and the anger that it evokes and turn up the compassion and understanding.

So, how can we tone down our anger? In Proverbs 15:1 it suggests, "A gentle answer turns away wrath, but a harsh word stirs up anger." If you become angry yourself, or are confronted by an angry person it is best not to throw gasoline on the fire. It is far better to throw some water on the fire with a gentle response to the anger at hand. In James 1:19-20 it says, "...Everyone should be quick to listen, slow to speak and slow to become angry, for man's anger does not bring about the righteous life that God desires."

Nobody likes to have people angry at them. I find it rather disturbing and unsettling. If someone is angry with me, I make it my number one priority to defuse the situation and smooth things out. In Matthew 5:9 Jesus says, "Blessed are the peacemakers, for they will be called sons of God." God prefers not to get angry. In Exodus 34:6 God says of himself, "...The Lord the Lord, the compassionate and gracious God, slow to anger abounding in love and faithfulness..."

Another way to put a lid on anger is to practice patience. Take a moment and think about how you would like to be treated if you made a mistake and made someone else angry. How would you like them to respond to you? In Ephesians 4:2 it says, "Be completely humble and patient, bearing with one another in love." We all mess up at times so let's try to be a little easier on one another and live more peacefully.

Peace

Have you ever been tormented by someone or something? You can't stop thinking about the situation and it begins intruding into your life and denying you sleep and joy and peace. If the torment persists for too long it can cause severe psychological problems. We are all fragile beings. It doesn't take much to push us over the edge. We all could use some help during these times.

I know how beautiful it is to live in peace. So, when my peace is shattered by some adverse situation or some unfortunate dispute with someone I try to resolve the situation as quickly as possible. In Psalms 34:14 it says, "Turn from evil and do good; seek peace and pursue it." Living in peace does not only produce happiness it also produces health. In Proverbs 14:30 it says, "A heart of peace gives life to the body..." So, fostering peace is good not only for our minds but our bodies as well. Studies have shown that stress causes high blood pressure and heart disease. The next time you get worked up; try to reach a peaceful resolution to your conflict as quickly as possible.

In Isaiah 48:22 it says, "There is no peace," says the lord, "for the wicked." I can attest to this. When I was leading a "wicked" life, I had no peace. I was tormented psychologically, I was under a great deal of stress and I was unhappy. True peace comes from God and God's peace is blissful. In Luke 2:14 it says, "Glory to God in the highest, and on earth peace to men on whom his favor rests." God grants peace to those who love Him and believe in Him and trust Him.

All good parents wish to see their children live a peaceful, productive and happy life. Our Father in heaven is the same way. He only wishes the best for his children. In John 14:27 Jesus says, "Peace I leave with you; my peace I give you. I do not give to you as the world gives. Do not let your hearts be troubled and do not be afraid." Jesus is saying that he does not give us "physical" gifts. So, don't ask Jesus for jet skis, wide screen TV's or new cars. Jesus gives us gifts that are far more valuable like peace of mind, wisdom, courage and eternal life.

Most of us have been around people who are constantly afraid or worried or totally pessimistic about life. I don't need to tell you that hanging out with these people can be a huge energy drain and a downright drag! We would all rather spend time with friends, office mates and family members who are at peace and happy with their lives. These people are way more fun to be around and we feel refreshed when we are around them. Jesus is the same way. Spending time getting to know Jesus will refresh you and change your outlook on the world. It will bring true peace into your life and you will never be the same.

Fear

Fear is debilitating. It stops us from doing things. There are all kinds of phobias that people have. These phobias can create tremendous fear. No matter what we are afraid of, we all know what it is like to be scared. We become frozen, our imaginations run away from us, our heart rate goes up and our skin begins to crawl. It's like entering another realm where our hearing becomes more focused and our reaction time quickens. A second stretches out to a minute and everything feels like it's moving in slow motion. Our thoughts are racing and our bodies are pumped up with adrenaline.

"Fight or flight?" No matter how disciplined you are or how much training you have had, you have no idea how you will react to a horrifying "real life" situation. Will you fight?

Will you flee? Or will you become frozen and vomit? These are all very human reactions. Each one of us has experienced and reacted to frightening situations. Life is scary sometimes! In Psalm 23:4 it says, "...Even though I walk through the valley of the shadow of death, I will fear no evil, for you are with me..." God is the antidote to fear.

In Psalm 56:3-4 it says, "When I am afraid, I will trust in you. In God whose word I praise, in God I trust; I will not be afraid." God is with us no matter where we go or what we do. He is our invisible 500 pound gorilla who is just waiting to pounce on any evil we may encounter. We have learned that through prayer, we can ask God for whatever we need. I pray daily for strength, courage and wisdom to deal with whatever comes my way in life. God has always been there to help me. In Hebrews 13:6 it says, "...The Lord is my helper, I will not be afraid..."

Have you ever seen the movie "Romancing the Stone"? There is a scene where Michael Douglas is taking a bus trip in Colombia. The bus suddenly stops and everyone gets out. The passengers exit the bus carrying their luggage with them and they start walking down the road. Michael Douglas is confused. The exact same thing happened to me. I was crossing the Andes in a bus when it stopped and everyone piled out and started walking away from the bus. I was confused as well. I asked the driver what was going on and he said that there was a landslide in the road. He told us that we would have to walk over the landslide and a bus would be waiting for us on the other side.

None of us were told about this when we bought tickets and we didn't have any choice but to do as he directed. I was traveling with a group of Americans and Canadians. There were about 10 of us traveling together. The soil was very soft and in some places we walked in other people's footsteps that were sunken about 18" in the ground. It was difficult walking for the first 15 minutes. When we reached the landslide, we were walking single file. The soil was firmer at this point and there was a 200 foot cliff to the left of us and a steep drop off to the right.

I was at the head of the line and I started to hear a rumbling noise coming from the plateau above us. I kept my eyes focused 200 feet above us as I walked. The rumbling grew louder and louder. Suddenly, I saw huge boulders and trees being pushed off the edge of the cliff above us. Instantly I yelled, "Run!" and took off sprinting for my life. Half the line followed me and the other half turned around and ran the other way. The last guy in my line was swallowed up by loose dirt from a mini-landslide caused by the debris that was pushed over the cliff. It carried him about 100 yards down the mountain.

The last guy in the line heading the other direction was knocked over and a boulder landed on his hand smashing his little finger. After the dust settled, we ran back to rescue the two most unfortunate guys in our traveling party. We dug out the guy who was buried and helped him up the mountain. He was badly shaken, but had no serious injuries. The other fellow's little finger was broken and the flesh on a quarter of his finger was gone. It was a bloody mess that exposed a portion of his finger bone. Fortunately, one of the women traveling with us was a nurse. She cleaned the wound as best as she could and bandaged it up.

After tending to the injured, we continued on our way in silence. About 45 minutes later, we came to a switchback in the road. There was a dump truck parked on the edge of the road. We walked around it, doubled back on the switch back and came around a blind turn where the road cut back to the left. A workman wearing a white hard hat walking in the opposite direction passed us by. I found this odd. I turned around and asked him what was going on ahead. The man yelled a one word answer over his shoulder without breaking his stride, "Dynamite!"

We all turned around immediately and headed back to where the worker stood. I went even further back to seek shelter next to the dump truck we had passed. About the time I arrived at the dump truck, there was an enormous explosion. The entire mountain side was blown up and parts of it were heading toward me! I dove under the truck and instantly heard the pinging of small rocks and debris hitting the parked vehicle.

Afterwards, I joined my traveling companions whose faces were still frozen in horror. I know what they were thinking. If I hadn't been prompted by the Holy Spirit to ask the worker what was going on, we would all have been dead! "Come on guys, we need to keep going otherwise we might miss the bus on the other side," I said. Again we walked in silence for another hour and finally saw a small canvas covered troop carrier waiting for us. We were exhausted as we piled in with all our gear. The driver took us to a clinic in town to have our friend's finger treated. In Isaiah 41:10 it says, "So do not fear, for I am with you; do not be dismayed, for I am your God. I will strengthen you and help you; I will uphold you with my righteous right hand."

Fear is an important emotion that alerts us to danger. It heightens our senses and boosts our physical strength. It's the body's way of getting our attention and focusing on the situation at hand. Unsubstantiated fear, lingering fear or excessive fear is unhealthy. It wears us down and weakens us. Learning to believe in God and trust in God can help us when we are facing a real life crisis. It can also help us eliminate unjustified fears. In John 4:18 it says, "There is no fear in love. But perfect love drives out fear…"

Dedication

This book is dedicated to all the Catholic sisters who have dedicated their own lives to serve Jesus Christ. Through your good work and dedication, you have made our world a better place. In Matthew 5:16 Jesus says, "...let your light shine before men, that they may see your good deeds and praise your Father in heaven." Thank you for the work you do.

67973345R00074

Made in the USA
Columbia, SC
02 August 2019